Christian
Meditation

The ks

Dom John Main, 1926-1982
Portrait by Brenda Bury

Christian Meditation

The Gethsemani Talks

John Main

Published by Medio Media

The Gethsemani Conferences were first published in three
consecutive issues of **Cistercian Studies** 1977-78

They are also available in French, German and
Portuguese translations.

ISBN 0-9666941-0-4

Library of Congress Catalog Number
98-89054

Drawings by Alba Taylor

Printed in USA

CONTENTS

TRINITY

INTRODUCTION

In November 1976 John Main was invited to speak to the Trappists of Gethsemani Abbey in Kentucky, Thomas Merton's monastery, on the subject of prayer. The talks he gave, published in this book, mark a historic moment in his own life as a teacher and in the spiritual history of our time.

There we can hear him as a monk speaking to monks about a monastic tradition. And yet this new edition of *The Gethsemani Talks* represents a spiritual teaching that has guided people in all walks of life and from many traditions for more than twenty years. These talks transmit a precious and ancient approach to prayer and spiritual practice that is universal in scope and relevance. But the tone of these talks is personal reminding us that essentially the spiritual tradition is an oral one, communicated from person to person.

So here, in a personally engaging way, John Main describes his own discovery of meditation, first through the East and later through his rediscovery of the Christian tradition in the teachings of the first Christian monks, the Desert Fathers. His own path of meditation then led him to a renewed understanding of the role of the monk in the modern world as a teacher and builder of bridges between spiritual traditions and between those traditions and the wastelands of contemporary materialism and anxiety. He became keenly aware of how relevant this simple practice of "pure prayer" could be for many seeking a purer depth of experience in their Christian faith and daily life. Still more radical perhaps, was his insight into meditation as a way of awakening the contemplative dimension in all areas of life and so of turning life into a search for the God who is seeking us. The meditator and the monk are in essence one.

The appeal and usefulness of this book, proven now for more

than twenty years, illustrates John Main's conviction that there is one essential Christian vocation. It is a call to radical discipleship: to make a total, self-transcending turn towards the Spirit in our heart. To meditate as a Christian, in John Main's view, is simply to live out the fullness of Christian discipleship in the depth of our being: to leave self behind and follow the master in his self-transcending return to the Father. To do this requires that we move from the mind to the heart, from intellectual belief to heart-felt faith. It is this deepening movement of consciousness which meditation initiates and steers which John Main called 'experience'. Tradition is the vitalizing and grounding context for the unfolding of this personal experience.

Twenty years have shown that John Main's emphasis on the need to return to experience, guided by tradition, touches the nerve of contemporary spirituality. The shallow rejection of the Christian tradition because of the institutional failures of Christianity or its foibles does immeasurable harm to the individuals and the culture who reject it. Seeing this the Dalai Lama advises people to remain seekers in their own tradition. But for many this is too hard to achieve without contact with the deeper reaches of this tradition and without a contemplative practice historically and theologically grounded in Christian faith.

This is what John Main has made readily available to so many. His understanding that contemplative experience breeds community – the genuine experience of *ecclesia* – has been illustrated in the continuing growth of the meditation community around the world. Myriad small weekly groups meeting in homes, churches, hospitals, schools and places of work; urban Christian meditation centres open to those of all traditions or none; the annual John Main Seminar led by Christian leaders in many fields from medicine to literature and once by the Dalai Lama; the inspiration shared from their contemplative practice between people working with the poor and for justice; the publishing company specializing in contemplative teaching – all this represents the fruits of meditation in the path which John Main opened up for or so many. And which he continues to do.

In this, his first public teaching on Christian meditation, John Main expresses the themes which the remaining years of his life would sound in the hearts of those he introduced to meditation. Above all, simplicity. For him meditation is simple. That is its appeal and its difficult challenge to modern people. We assume that simple means easy and quick. John Main prefers to speak of meditation as a discipline rather than as a technique or method in order to dispel this illusion. He identified, like the masters before him, what are the primary obstacles to reaching this simplicity. There is above all our chronic state of distractedness but behind that our habitual egotism and self-centredness. Only simplicity can simply. Only purity can purify. And so the mantra, Cassian's 'formula', is the sacrament of this simplicity which leads the meditator into the gospel beatitude of poverty of spirit and purity of heart.

The modern search for spirituality shows that people are seeking a new way of life that is integrated, balanced and authentically in touch with all aspects of their humanity. John Main shows that this is a wise and achievable goal but that it requires more than good will. It asks for commitment to the inner journey of simplifying the mind and purifying the heart. The fruits of meditation, he then assures us, will make themselves evident in the changes wrought in our personality and in all our responses to the world. Above all it is our relationships, where self and other meet in the mystery of love and transcendence that we see why the discipline, freely followed, leads to the liberty of love. This beautiful vision is rooted in the ordinary daily practice of meditation and in his understanding that the two periods of meditation each day uncover and set flowing the river of prayer which is ever-present within us, the stream of 'living water' which Jesus proclaimed as the essential truth of human nature. Like the generations of monks before him John Main knew that the discipline of daily periods of prayer lead to the state of continuous and unbroken prayer.

Other books and many tapes by John Main followed the opening of his public teaching on meditation at Gethsemani. They remain ever-fresh and inspiring to a new generation excited by his steady focus, his clarity and his strong spiritual gentleness. But *The Gethsemani Talks* prove that what he said later in so many ways is essentially simple and can be said clearly and in few words. This little book therefore remains the best introduction to meditation in the Christian tradition and to the charm of John Main's own spirit and style as a teacher.

Laurence Freeman
International Centre
The World Community for Christian Meditation
November 1998

FIRST CONFERENCE

In the first of his talks to the community,

Dom John spoke of his own initiation into meditation.

FATHER

My dearest brothers in St. Benedict: in these talks I am hoping to share with you an understanding and an experience of prayer which is something fuller than a mere *theory* of prayer. It seems to me that the impersonal theory, however *right*, is forever floating in the stratosphere. To be brought down to earth it needs to be given its personal context and it then has a claim to be not only *right* but *true* as well.

I was first introduced to meditation long before I became a monk, when I was serving in the British Colonial Service in Malaya. My teacher was an Indian swami who had a temple just outside Kuala Lumpur. When I first met him on some official business or other I was deeply impressed by his peacefulness and calm wisdom. I was pleased to see that he seemed willing to talk on a personal level once our business was concluded and we fell into conversation. He then asked me if I was a religious man. I told him I was a Catholic. He then asked me if I meditated. I told him I tried to and, at his bidding, described briefly what we have come to know as the Ignatian method of meditation. He was silent for a short time and then gently remarked that his own tradition of meditation was quite different. For the swami, the aim of meditation was the coming to awareness of the Spirit of the universe who dwells in our hearts and he recited these verses from the Upanishads: "He contains all things, all works and desires and all perfumes and tastes. And he enfolds the whole universe and, in silence, is loving to all. This is the Spirit that is in my heart. This is Brahman."

The swami read this passage with such devotion and such meaning that I asked him if he would accept me as a pupil to teach me how to meditate in his way. He replied: "Meditation is very simple ... all you have to do is to meditate. If you would like to learn I will try to teach you. What I suggest is this ... that you come out and meditate with me once a week. Before we meditate I will tell you a few things but the important thing is that we meditate together."

I began to visit the holy man regularly and this is what he told me on my first visit. He said: "To meditate you must become silent. You must be still. And you must concentrate. In our tradition we know one way in which you can arrive at that stillness, that concentration. We use a *word* that we call a *mantra*. To meditate, what you must do is to choose this word and then repeat it, faithfully, lovingly and continually. That is all there is to meditation. I really have nothing else to tell you. And now we will meditate."

And so, every week for about 18 months, I went out to this holy man of God, sat down beside him and meditated with him for half an hour. He told me that provided I was serious in my quest – it was absolutely necessary to meditate twice a day for half an hour and to meditate twice a day, every day. He said: "Meditating only when you come out to see me will be a frivolity. Meditating once a day will be frivolity. If you are serious and if you want to root this mantra in your heart then this is the minimum undertaking ... that you meditate first thing in the morning for half an hour and sometime in the evening for half an hour. And during the time of your meditation there must be in your mind no thoughts, no words, no imaginations. The sole sound will be the sound of your mantra, your word. The mantra (he continued) is like a harmonic. And as we sound this harmonic within ourselves we begin to build up a resonance. That resonance then leads us forward to our own wholeness ... We begin to experience the deep unity we all possess in our own being. And then the harmonic begins to build up a resonance between you and all creatures and all creation and a unity between you and your Creator."

I would often ask the swami: "How long will this take? How long will it take me to achieve enlightenment?" But the swami would either ignore my crassness or else would reply with the words that really sum up his teaching and wisdom: "Say your mantra". In all those eighteen months this was the essential core of everything he had to say: "Say your mantra".

On my return to Europe to teach Law at Trinity College, Dublin, years before the advent of the Beatles and the discovery of T.M., I found no one who really knew about meditation as I now understand it. I first tried to raise the subject with priest-friends but to my surprise my inquiries were mostly received with great suspicion and sometimes even hostility.

As far as I could gather from my conversation these good men practiced very faithfully a Jesuit-type of meditation and the best among them prepared for their morning mental prayer by systematically going through a list of points for the morning. To me it seemed very esoteric and somewhat complicated.

The book that seemed to have the greatest influence among these very sincere men was Dom Chautard's *The Soul of the Apostolate*, which had, I gathered, been widely recommended in the seminaries in the 1930's. It was a book that struck me as rather complex.

But for me personally there was all the joy and excitement of the pilgrimage of my morning and evening meditation. All the time there was a growing attraction to meditation and the morning and evening times became the real axis on which my day was built.

About this time, 1958, a nephew of mine, one of my sister's children, became seriously ill and died. The death of this child had an enormous effect on me and brought me face to face with the questions of life and death and the whole purpose of existence. As I reviewed my life at this time I was forcibly struck by the fact that the most important thing in my entire existence was my daily meditation. I decided, therefore, to structure my life on my meditation and sought to do so by becoming a monk.

On becoming a monk, however, I was given another method

of meditation which I accepted in obedience in my new status as a Benedictine novice. This new method was the so-called "prayer of acts" – that is, a half hour spent in acts of adoration, contrition, thanskgiving and supplication, a half hour, that is to say, of prayer that was largely words addressed to God in the heart and thoughts about God in the mind. I accepted this development with the same kind of fatalism behind Alexander Pope's: "Whatever is, is right." I waited and postponed any serious confrontation with the fact that this new form of prayer was becoming more and more unsatisfactory. And, of course, as I became more and more busy as a monk this fact became less and less urgent.

In retrospect I regard this period in my life as one of great grace. Unwittingly my novice master had set out to teach me detachment at the very centre of my life. I learned to become detached from the practice that was most sacred to me and on which I was seeking to build my life.

Instead I learned to build my life on God himself. The next few years were bleak years in terms of spiritual development but I always went back to the obedience which was the foundation of my life as a monk. I think too that somewhere deep inside of me there was a faith that God would not leave me forever wandering in the wilderness and would call me back on to the path. What was important was that I should come back on his terms and not on my own.

Finally, there came a stage in this retrogression when everything seemed set for an eternal postponement of any urgent action in getting back to a more vital life of prayer. I became headmaster of St. Anselm's School in Washington, D.C., and was plunged into the busiest time I have ever had in my monastic life. The urgent issues were the raising of money for a new science wing, college placement, examination ratings. In the midst of all this, however, a young man came to the monastery asking to be taught something about

Christian mysticsm. He had spent some time with a Hindu teacher
but was now looking for the Christian standpoint. So, with some
malice aforethought, I gave him Baker's *Holy Wisdom* as his first book
of study, thinking that this would keep him quietly occupied for
several weeks, unravelling its loping, Drydenesque sentences. To
my amazement, however, he reacted with real and immediate en-
thusiasm, to such a degree that I felt I had to read it again myself.
We began to read it together and very soon afterwards we also
began to meditate together.

In Baker I rediscovered a sense of the wonder of the monastic
vocation which years of mere busyness had dulled, together with a
glimmering understanding of prayer in its simplicity and its present
reality. In Baker, too, there is an intuitive understanding of the mantra in those passages dealing with "acts" and "those which are com-
monly called ejaculatory prayers".[1] He writes with both the confidence and appeal of a man who has recognised the wrong turnings
that have somehow brought him back to the right path. He writes
with authority:

> "Certain it is that vocal prayers though never so pro-
> longed and in never so great solitude, yet will never pro-
> duce this effect (of recollectedness) where the true spirit
> of contemplative prayer is not known, and such ignorance
> hath been even in orders of the greatest abstraction and
> austerity; thus we see that Germanus and Cassianus,
> though practised many years in a strict cenobitical life,
> yet were astonished when they heard the holy hermits
> discourse of pure spiritual prayer, free from images".[2]

Baker's frequent reminder of the emphatic insistence St.
Benedict lays upon Cassian's Conferences sent me to them seriously
for the first time. It was with very wonderful astonishment that I
read, in his Tenth Conference, of the practice of using a single short

---

1   Holy Wisdom (Burns & Oates 1964) p. 321
2   ibid.

phrase to achieve the stillness necessary for prayer;

> "The mind thus casts out and represses the rich and
> ample matter of all thoughts and restricts itself to the pov-
> erty of a single verse".[3]

In reading these words in Cassian and Chapter X of the same Conference on the method of continual prayer, I was arrived home once more and returned to the practice of the mantra.

The story of John Cassian and his friend, Germanus, no less than the teaching and wisdom of the Conferences themselves, have a striking contemporary relevance. Like many thousands of modern Westerners looking and travelling to the East these two young monks of the fourth century wanted above all to learn to pray and they suffered restlessness while they looked for a teacher. They first went to the monastery in Bethlehem in search of a living tradition but suffered grievous loss from the mediocrity of the manner of life there"[4] and, as St. Jerome arrived with his accompanying storms of intellectual controversy, they obtained permission to set off to the Egyptian desert. In the Ninth Conference, Cassian describes their visit to Abba Isaac and their appeal to him to tell them about prayer. Isaac responded and spoke to them evidently from the heart, not with any mere theory. He spoke out of his own experience, his own distilled wisdom – a wisdom learnt in constant faithfulness to prayer and vigils.

Cassian and Germanus listened with growing rapture to the holy man as they realised that they had found their teacher and as they listened their hearts burned within them as he spoke to them of ceaseless prayer. Their response was wholehearted: This is what we must do! We ourselves must in our own lives practise this continual recollection of the holy presence of God. We must achieve in our lives what this holy man has done in his. With this fervent spirit awakened in them they take their leave of Isaac and are returning to

3   Cassian Conference X (xi)
4   Conf. XVII (x)

their own cell when they stop in their tracks. They say to each other what many have said since: We know that prayer is the only thing! We know that we want to pray. We know that the Spirit of Him who raised Jesus from the dead dwells within us and will give new life to our mortal bodies. We "know" all that! (We wouldn't have come all this way if we had not known it.) But what the holy abbot did not tell us was: How are we going to do it? How are we going to achieve this continual recollection and prayer?

So they returned to Isaac and with a respectful tone tinged with impatience they said: "You discoursed to us eloquently and with love on the subject of prayer and you have almost blinded us with your golden words! But what you did not tell us is how are we going to do it."

Isaac's response to this burst of youthful idealism is at the same time encouraging and tempering. He gives the impression of having actually foreseen it, indeed of having tested the true seriousness of their intent and so:

"I do not think I shall have any difficulty in introducing you into what I may call the hall (of prayer) for you to roam about its recesses as the Lord may direct ... For he is next door to understanding who carefully recognizes what he ought to ask about, nor is he far from knowledge who begins to understand how ignorant he is".[5]

Cassian subtly creates the necessary context for Abbot Isaac's revelation in the opening chapters of the Conference. He opens it with a solemn pronouncement that the "doctrine" to be expounded is "so important that men cannot be ignorant of it without terrible blasphemy and serious harm to the Catholic faith".[6]

This solemn doctrine is charmingly personalized in the ensuing story of Abbot Serapion.

5   Conf. X (ix)
6   ibid. Introduction

Serapion was one of the elders of the desert community who had been long fallen into the heresy of Anthropomorphism – that is, he had made God in his own image and likeness. Cassian's point is that this is the great danger for all Christian prayer: that we cut God down to our own size in order to talk to Him, making a convenient shoulder for us to cry on and a convenient idol enabling us to avoid the abyss of His otherness. What we should be understanding, on the other hand, is both His utter transcendence and His utter closeness to us in His indwelling Spirit. It is to this understanding of prayer that Serapion is now led by the learned Photinus – the Serapion whose 40 years of ascetic ordeal in the desert have not succeeded in leading him out of the unnecessary wilderness of Anthropomorphism. Again, it is not by theory but practice that Serapion is initiated into what Cassian keeps calling the "Catholic" way of prayer[7] – prayer without images, that restricts itself to the repetition of a single verse, the "prayer of poverty". Cassian tells us that when the other hermits in the desert heard that Serapion had been converted to the prayer of the Catholic faith, they all came to pray with him and rejoiced. But Serapion himself bursts into tears and cries pitifully:

> "They have taken my God from me and I have now none to lay hold of, and who to worship and address I know not."[8]

It is proof of Cassian's subtlety that he places this story at the head of the Conference. It first of all brings theory to earth in the moving story of Serapion's conversion. More importantly, it emphasises that no human consideration can obscure the utter transcendence of God and the essential place this knowledge must hold in our understanding of prayer. It shows us the reverence we must bring to prayer. And it shows us, above all, that in all prayer it is the Lord God Himself who is the prime mover – His first movement being to send us His Son, Jesus. So if we are truly within Cassian's

7   ibid. (iii)
8   ibid.

"Catholic tradition" we begin to apprehend that Christian prayer is in essence disposing ourselves so that the murmur of the prayer of Jesus may arise in our hearts.

Then Cassian reports Isaac's instruction on the way in which we are to say this mantra, this verse. And the verse that he recommends is: *"Deus in adjutorium meum intende,"* which St. Benedict thought so highly of that he had us begin each of our Offices with it. Of the mantra Cassian says this:

> "This mantra must always be in your heart. When you go to sleep let it be saying this verse till having been moulded by it you grow accustomed to repeat it even in your sleep".[9]

On rising it should "anticipate all your waking thoughts" and throughout the day it should be singing ceaselessly in "the recesses of the heart".

The metaphor of a pilgrimage is one that often occurs to us as we reflect on our life or even specific areas of our life. It is one that well describes the roundabout way in which Augustine Baker found his entry into the tradition of Christian prayer, no less than it describes the physical undertaking of Cassian and Germanus in their journey to the Egyptian desert. But each and every one of us is called to follow this same pilgrimage to uncover the prayer of Jesus within our heart.

All that I have said to you this evening is what I have been able to discover in my own limited experience. I am not suggesting for a moment that this is the only way there is to pray. There are, of course, many mansions in the Father's kingdom. But it is the only way I have been able to discover and it is a way that is of great simplicity. All you have to do is to find your word, ideally with the help of a teacher, and then faithfully to repeat it. But don't let me mislead

9   ibid. (xiv)

you. Actually to say the word morning and evening, day in and day out, winter and summer, whether you feel like it or don't feel like it, all this requires a good deal of grit, determination and steel in the spine. Remember Serapion. But if you can say it, I think it will bring you to an understanding of your monastic life that will bring it incredible richness.

If I may, I would like to end with this short excerpt from Scripture:

> "With this in mind, then, I kneel in prayer to the Father from whom every family in heaven and on earth takes its name, that out of the treasures of his glory he may grant you strength and power through his Spirit in your inner being, that through faith Christ may dwell in your hearts in love. With deep roots and firm foundations, may you be strong to grasp with all God's people what is the breadth and length and height and depth of the love of Christ and to know it, though it is beyond knowledge. So may you attain to fullness of being, the fullness of God himself."[10]

10 Eph. 3:14-19

SECOND CONFERENCE

**In his second talk, Dom John spoke of
meditation as the way of personally verifying
the truth of our faith.**

SON

I n this talk this evening, my dear brothers, I would like to share with you what I have experienced in my own life of the truths of our religion through the sort of meditation I spoke to you of last evening.

God is our Creator and Father. Jesus is our Redeemer and Brother. And the Holy Spirit dwells within each one of us in such a way that we are – as we heard in the beautiful Liturgy of Vespers this evening – we are all of us, quite literally "temples of holiness". Now meditation is simply the process whereby we come to terms with these truths: truths about God, truths about ourselves, truths, too, about our neighbour. For in our daily meditations we stand aside from all that we can bring together under the term "ephemeral immediacy and we open ourselves fully to the grandeur and the wonder of God – to the enduring present. And in this process we both discover our own grandeur and liberate our capacity for wonder. We might equally well say that in discovering our own value we discover God, the Creator of all that is valuable. We discover, with Gerard Manley Hopkins, that the world "is charged with the grandeur of God".[11]

The key word in what I have just said is "liberate". Meditation is a process of liberation: we must set these truths free in our lives. And it seems to me, my dearest brothers, that as Christians we have so often lived our lives on a merely propositional basis. The framework of our response to God has, as a result, been so incomplete, so narrowly rational: a mere compendium of creeds and formulas. But in meditative prayer we prepare for the full experience of the personal presence of Jesus within us, this *pleroma* being the personal presence of the Father, the Son and the Holy Spirit – the whole life of the most Holy Trinity lived out within us.

Now this is just the sort of proposition that we must set free within our hearts: set free from its merely theological or rhetorical formulation so that it lives, enriches and transforms our lives and

11 "God's Grandeur"

does this, in the words of St. Peter, at "the inmost centre of our being".[12] And so, meditation is also a learning process. It is the process of learning to pay attention, to concentrate. We have to *attend* both in the English sense of the word of *paying attention* and in the French sense of *waiting*. We have all to learn this one fundamental lesson if we are ever going to discover the full riches of our Christian faith, the richness of our intimate relation and involvement with Jesus.

In meditation, then, we learn to pay attention to the personal presence of Jesus within us. We begin to learn this by learning to be undistracted, to be at peace and to enjoy to the full the wonder of our creation. We are then learning to sing with the psalmist from the fullness of our heart: "I thank you for the wonder of my being".[13]

I want to try to emphasise for you, dear brothers, a truth that so often escapes us in the practical reality of our daily lives – daily lives that are so often filled with mere busyness. It is the fundamental truth that each one of us is created by God; that each one of us has, therefore, a Divine origin. Now this is so rudimentary a proposition of our faith and one that we, most of us, learned by rote at a very early age that we tend never to *realise* it fully, to set it free from all the abstraction of the stale proposition and to allow it to serve its real purpose in activating our spirit. I think it was something like this that he had in mind when the author wrote this energetic exhortation to the Hebrews:

> "Let us then stop discussing the rudiments of Christianity. We ought not to be laying over again the foundations of faith in God ... Instead, let us advance towards maturity, and so we shall if God permits." [14]

If people were to reflect – not propositionally but directly – on their Divine origin they could hardly fail to grow daily in the sense, however dimly, of the wondrous ambience within which we all have our being. And the wondrous quality of our being's not lessened or

12 I Pet. 3:4
13 Psalm 138:14
14 Heb. 6:1-3

threatened but unimaginably heightened by the infinite power and wonder of God, our Creator. This truth alone would be enough to sustain us in worshipful awe for a lifetime. But in the revelation of Jesus, our Redeemer, our Brother, we discover that not only do we have this Divine origin but that we also share, are called to share, in His own nature and being. We have then, each one of us equally and uniquely, an infinite importance and an infinite value. We have not only been created out of nothing by God but we have, each one of us, been redeemed, liberated, by His Son, Jesus. And then, as a permanent guarantee of our origin and as a permanent guarantee of our importance and value, Jesus has sent his Spirit to dwell within us, making all of us temples of holiness: God himself dwelling within us.

The "maturity" that the author exhorted the Hebrews to attain was far from being the discursive elaboration of propositions, "the rudiments of Christianity" as he called them. It was rather the liberation from the inevitable limitations and distortions of the merely propositional. And this maturity develops, he continued:

> "When men have once been enlightened, when they have had a taste of the heavenly gift and a share in the Holy Spirit, when they have experienced the goodness of God's word and the spiritual energies of the age to come . . ."[15]

Now we are all of us only too familiar with these truths on the level of theological theory. But in meditation we seek to live with these truths in practice – or, perhaps more accurately: we seek to *live* these truths. Meditative prayer is not an intellectual exercise in which we reflect about theological propositions. In meditation we are not *thinking* about God at all, nor are we thinking of His Son, Jesus, nor of the Holy Spirit. In meditation we seek to do something immeasurably greater: we seek to *be with* God, to *be with* Jesus, to *be with* His Holy Spirit; not merely to think about them. It is one thing to

15 Heb. 6:4-6

know that Jesus is the revelation of the Father; it is one thing to know that Jesus is our way to the Father. But it is quite another thing to experience the presence of Jesus within us, to experience the power of His Spirit within us; and *in that experience* to be brought into the presence of His Father and our Father.

When we reflect about our creature status, the status that is our human condition, we begin to see that prayer – which is our paying attention to this fundamental relationship of Creator / creature in our lives is not just a peripheral or optional activity: nor is it just a duty. Prayer is the fundamental and grounding experience of everything we are. In other words, prayer is the process wherein we discover both who we are and why we are. In essence, it is the process whereby and wherein we pay attention with total concentration to our own human nature so that, by attending to our own creatureliness, we come to attend to and upon our Creator. St. Augustine put this very succinctly and very marvellously in this way:

"Man must first be restored to himself, that, making
in himself as it were a stepping-stone, he may rise thence
and be borne up to God".[16]

So prayer, meditation, is not just a way of "doing" something but it is a way of "becoming" someone – becoming yourself: created by God, redeemed by Jesus and a temple of the Holy Spirit.

And so, dearest brothers, in meditation we go beyond thoughts, even holy thoughts. Meditation is concerned not so much with thinking as with being. And in contemplative prayer we seek to become the person we are called to be: not by thinking about God but by being with Him. Simply to be in His presence is all-sufficing. Simply to be with Him is to be drawn into being the person He calls us to be. This is the message of Jesus' injunction to seek the kingdom first and then all else will be given. But this is no easy task for those of us reared in our contemporary western culture. We have all been

16 Retractions I (viii) 3 (Migne PL XXXII)

conditioned by this culture's excessive regard for cerebral activity. And we have defined ourselves far too narrowly as "rational creatures". It seems to me that this is one of the principal reasons for the impoverishment of our prayer life. The response of the *whole person* to God has been shattered and only the cerebral, verbal splinters are active in our very much attenuated understanding of prayer. Our aim in Christian prayer is to allow God's mysterious and silent presence within us to become more and more not only a reality, one of several to which we give what Cardinal Newman called "notional assent", but the reality which gives meaning, shape and purpose to everything we do, to everything we are. And so, prayer is not the time for words, however beautifully and sincerely phrased. All our words are wholly ineffective when we enter into mysterious communion with God whose Word is before and after all other words.

In prayer, then, we seek the way of simplicity. And this is what in my own experience I have discovered as the way of the mantra. Listen to John Cassian again:

> "This is the formula which the mind could unceasingly cling to until, strengthened by the constant use of it and by continual meditation, it casts off and rejects the rich and ample matter of all manner of thoughts and restricts itself to the poverty of a single verse".[17]

What I am suggesting to you is that there is a real danger for the religious man – and indeed all men – of living our lives by responding merely to propositions rather than by deepening our own awareness and apprehension of and commitment to, living and self-authenticating truth. There is a very real danger for us religious men that we can so easily become smug and self-complacent as we repeat our credal formulas. Rather as the political man can rest easy *talking* about liberty, fraternity and equality. And the result of this excessive intellectualisation of our lives is that in so many cases we are only half alive. Or to put it in its less palatable form: We are half

17 Conference X (xi)

dead. As the women of Canterbury put it in Eliot's "Murder in the Cathedral", itself a vision of half-life that led to death:

> "And meanwhile we have gone on living,
> Living and partly living,
> Picking together the pieces ..."

Now what is the way forward? Curiously, paradoxically it is the way of poverty. All Christians are called to live out a certain spirit of poverty in their lives: that is to say that all of us are called to that degree of selflessness which will enable us to be fully and deply sensitive to the reality of the *other* – God, our neighbour. And this, so it seems to me, is what religious poverty is concerned with: a lived acknowledgment of the wonder of God in all his glory. And at the same time an acknowledgment that all our being is a sharing in and reflection of His Being. This is a notion that we need to consider afresh, to make real in our real lives. We have so often in the past spoken of poverty in merely negative terms, merely as renunciation, when we should have pondered and realised the unimaginable richness of Christian poverty – in which we become as John Cassian himself puts it "grandly poor".[18] By our lived poverty we admit, both affirming and welcoming, the truth of God's richness and glory. And in this admission, this affirmation and acceptance, we are, each one of us, made aware that our own true richness and glory lies in him and not in mere possessions. The spirit of poverty, then, in the deepest sense is an affirmation of our own infinite value. We are the valued subjects of God's love.

Now the vow of poverty that we as monks take commits us to an enduring experience of God which runs far deeper into our life than the mere renunciation of personal property. The poverty that we as religious promised to pursue and experience is only signalled and symbolised by our detachment from money and material possessions. The real poverty we must practice is an impoverishment of isolating selfishness: the real renunciation is of all the alienating

18 ibid.

tendencies of a materialism which can so easily build barriers around each one of us – barriers just as real as the thick walls of a medieval town or the barbed wire of a security guarded suburban compound. Behind these self isolating barriers we can seem so safe. And yet our security is not that which derives from acceptance, from living in harmony with our environment, with our neighbours. But it is a security ultimately dependent on sustained rejection and repulsion, indicated by the violence we are prepared to turn on all those who threaten our isolation. But what, you will say, has this to do with meditation? In meditation, in meditative, contemplative prayer, we seek to practice the basic poverty – in John Cassian's words: "restricting the activity of our mind to the poverty of a single verse" – the mantra. And Cassian's clear assertion is this: that *thereby* we discover the infinite riches of God. Then, our "security" is not built on negative forces but rooted in the one positive force in the cosmos, the Lord God himself, known and experienced, in the love of Jesus. That is the bedrock of all Christian confidence and courage which gave authority to the words and works of Jesus.

We must therefore take extreme care about using terms like "self-renunciation". In prayer we do truly seek to turn our whole being to a contemplation of God's goodness, of his infinite love. But we can only do this with any degree of effectiveness when we have first truly come close to ourselves. Prayer itself is the way to experience the truth of the words of Jesus: "The man who would find his life, must first lose it".[19] But we have to take a preliminary step. And this first step is to gain the necessary confidence to lay down our life in the poverty of this single verse in meditation. This is the tremendous importance of Christian community – when we live with brothers and experience ourselves as revered and loved we build up the confidence that is necessary to enter into prayer where we practice this total poverty, this total renunciation. And Christian self-renunciation is always a self-affirmation in Christ.

19 Mt. 10:39 (RSV)

Meditation and the poverty of it is no form of self rejection. We are not running away from ourselves, nor do we hate ourselves. On the contrary, our search is a search for ourselves and the experience of our own personal and infinite capacity to be loved. The harmony of the real Self that lies beyond all selfishness, beyond all ego-based activity is so well attested to in the Christian tradition. St. Catherine of Genoa put it succinctly: "My *me* is God. Nor do I know my selfhood save in him."[20] But to *arrive* at our selfhood – and it is to that invitation we respond when we meditate – or, putting it in the more felicitous and perhaps more accurate language of the East, to *realise* ourselves – we must pass into the radical experience of personal poverty with an unflinching self-surrender.

And what we surrender, what we die to is, in the thought of Zen, not the self or the mind but rather that *image* of the self or the mind which we have mistakenly come to identify with who we really are. Now this is not a proposition that we need in the language of the *Cloud*, "to expound with imaginative cleverness".[21] But it does indicate that what we are renouncing in prayer is, essentially, *unreality*. And the pain of the renunciation will be in proportion to the extent that we have committed ourselves to unreality, the extent to which we have taken our illusions to be real. In prayer we divest ourselves of the illusion of the isolating ego: we do so in a sustained act of Faith by concentrating our entire self away from the *idea* of ourselves, by concentrating on the real Self, created by God, redeemed by Jesus, a temple of the Holy Spirit.

We must first then come near to ourselves by finding our own true Self. But we have still to learn to enter into the paradox that Jesus put before us: "The man who would find his life *(psyche)* must first lose it". Meditation is the prayer of Faith because we are willing to follow the Teacher's command: we are willing to lose our lives so that we may realise fully our own potential.

And when we have found our true Self, our task is as it were

20 Quoted E. Underhill "The Mystics of the Church" (Clarke, London 2nd Ed.) p. 51
21 Cloud of Unknowing (Penguin Books 1961) Ch. 36

only beginning. For as soon as we have found ourselves what we have done – again in St. Augustine's expression – is to have found the essential "steppingstone" that will lead us to God. Because then – and only then – do we find the confidence necessary to take the next step, which is to stop looking at our new-found Self, to turn the searchlight off ourselves and onto the Other. And meditation is the prayer of Faith precisely because we leave ourselves behind *before* the Other appears, and with no pre-packaged guarantee that he will appear. The essence of all poverty consists in this risk of annihilation.

This is the leap of faith from ourselves to the Other – and it is the risk involved in all loving. Now only a little experience of the practice of meditation reveals for you that the process of self-impoverishment is a continuous and continually more radical experience. And this is a delicate moment in our development of prayer. For when we begin to realise the totality of the commitment involved in deep, self-surrendering prayer, there is a strong temptation to turn back, to evade the call to total poverty, to give up meditation, to give up the ascesis of the mantra and to return to self-centred rather than God-centred prayer.

The temptation is to return to that prayer we might describe as the prayer of anaesthetised, floating piety – the prayer that John Cassian termed the *"pax perniciosa"* (the ruinous peace) and the *"sopor letalis"* (the lethal sleep). [22] This is a temptation we have to transcend. Jesus has called us to *lose* our life; not to lend it, not to hold out negotiating for better terms. If we lose it and *only* if we lose it will we find it in him. And the vision of prayer of John Cassian, restricting our mind to one word is proof of the genuineness of our renunciation. In his vision of prayer we renounce thought, imagination, even self-consciousness itself; the matrix of language and reflection.

But let us be quite clear why we renounce all these gifts of God

22 Conference X (viii)

at the time of prayer, at what the author of the *Cloud* calls "the time of the work". It would not be enough to say that we renounce them merely because they "distract". It would indeed be absurd for us to deny that they are the primary natural means of self understanding and communication. Nor do we renounce them because we consider that they have no place in either our social or personal relationship with God. It is obvious that the whole of our liturgical response to God is based on word, gesture and image. And Jesus himself has told us that we can pray to the Father in his name for whatever we need, for the needs of the whole world.

All these considerations must constantly be kept sight of. But at the centre of our being I think all of us know the truth of what Jesus means when he invites us to lose our lives so that we may find them. At this same centre we, all of us, feel the need for a radical simplicity, a moving beyond all our activities to the unitary principle of activity itself: the cause and end of movement. In other words, we all know the need we have to rejoice in our being at its simplest, where it simply exists with no reason for its existence other than that it gives glory to God who created it, who loves it and who sustains it in being. And it is in prayer that we experience the sheer joy that there is in simple being. Having surrendered everything we have, everything by which we exist or know that we exist, we stand before the Lord God in utter simplicity. And the poverty of the single verse that John Cassian enjoins is the means in meditation of losing our life that we may find it, of becoming nothing that we may become the All.

THIRD CONFERENCE

**In his third conference
Dom John answered questions
put to him by the community**

SPIRIT

*D*om *John:* Now, my dear brothers, it's a little difficult to know how to proceed on an occasion like this because I sometimes find that if I ask for questions a great silence ensues. Maybe that won't be the case with you. But I thought a useful way of proceeding would be if I gave you just a very short synopsis of what I've been trying to put before you – on the basis that the best teacher tells his students what he is going to tell them, then tells them, then tells them what he's told them!

So, very briefly, as I understand it, all Christian prayer is a growing awareness of God in Jesus. And for that growing awareness we need to come to a state of undistraction, to a state of attention and concentration – that is, to a state of awareness. And as far as I have been able to determine in the limitations of my own life, the only way that I have been able to find to come to that quiet, to that undistractedness, to that concentration, is the way of the mantra.

Now I'd just like to make one point very clear and it's this: as far as I can understand him, St. Benedict saw the monastic life in terms of *oratio* (prayer), *lectio* (reading) and *labor* (work) – all bound together and harmonised by love, mutual charity. What I have been talking to you about the last couple of days concerns the *oratio* but, of course, the other two components are essential; particularly the *lectio*, the reading of the Bible and the New Testament above all, is fundamental for a complete Christian response. And as far as the *oratio* is concerned, there is more than one form of Christian prayer. We have our liturgical prayer together, we have the vocal prayer that we quite naturally engage in and then we have our more strictly contemplative prayer. What I have found in my own limited experience about the relationship of these forms of our participation in the prayer of Jesus is this: as I have over the years practised the form of meditation I've been speaking to you about, the Divine Office has become ever more of a delight and less of a duty.

I think this happens because, as I have been suggesting to you in these talks, meditation progressively opens up for us the *reality* of our faith. When Carl Jung was once asked in an interview whether he believed in God he paused for a few moments and then very gently and simply replied: "No. *I know."* Cassian, at the end of his Second Conference of Abbot Isaac, is getting at the same thing when he emphasises the way that meditation leads us into a world of direct experience. For example, he says, in reading the Psalms we no longer just read them or memorise them, we come to "get at their meaning not by reading the text but by experience and anticipating it". And the sense of the words of Scripture, he says, is not revealed by a commentary on them as much as by what he calls "practical proof" because our own experience exposes the very veins and marrow of the Word of God.

Walter Hilton is a very good witness that there is no antipathy as it were between contemplative prayer, vocal prayer, liturgical prayer. He does trace a kind of progressive development through these forms but not in the sense that we ever get to a stage in our life when we have *gone beyond* liturgical prayer or vocal prayer. The development he really sees is a growth in the delight with which one enters into whatever form is appropriate at any time. And all these forms of prayer are, of course, complementary, provided that we know them as they really are: as entrances into the eternal prayer of Jesus which is his loving return to the Father. At all times in our lives all the various streams of prayer are coming together and binding us ever more closely to the Lord Jesus in the universal ocean of his prayer.

If we can see prayer in this context we are, I think, on the way to transcending our obstructive self-consciousness about it, about forms or techniques. One must be especially careful when one comes to consider the form of prayer I have been describing of not getting sidetracked by thinking about the technique. There could hardly be anything more simple than taking a single word like "Jesus" or

"Abba". But sometimes when people hear about meditation for the first time they miss the simplicity which is the essence and become fixated on what they see as some kind of esoteric, foreign prayer technique. When we're trying to teach this to lay people in Europe or America we find they often get quite confused when they hear of it for the first time and the message we find most difficult to convey – the only message there is to convey – is that there is not need for confusion because all is simplicity itself.

We had a dear Irish lady come to one of our groups a few months ago and I explained to them briefly what had to be done. And I told them that the mantra that I recommend is "Maranatha". I recommend it because it is in Aramaic, the language Jesus himself spoke, because it's probably the most ancient prayer in the Church: St. Paul ends Corinthians with it, John ends Revelation with it, it can be found in the Didache – and so forth. Throughout the *Cloud of Unknowing* the author urges us to choose a word that is full of meaning; but that once you have chosen it, to turn from the meaning and associations and to listen to it as a sound. "Maranatha" is a perfect mantra from that point of view. Anyway, this good lady listened to all this and then we went in and meditated. And when we came out she said, "Oh, Father, a dreadful thing happened once I got into the meditation room: didn't I forget the mantra!". And she said: "I sat there and I thought, how can I meditate if I hadn't the mantra? But, Father, God is good; didn't I remember it after a few minutes: Macooshla, Macooshla!."

So the mantra is a very, very simple device that is meant to bring you in all simplicity into the presence of your Lord. If you'd like to ask any questions now we might try to move forward.

Question: How important was it to meditate in the first instance with your teacher, your guru, the holy Hindu Swami?

Dom John: It was certainly a very great help to me. He was a man of very deep and very evident holiness and power, and just to be with him was to know that you were in the presence of the power of a really radiant human being. And I think there is no doubt that this is the greatest need that the Church has today: a sufficiency of men of his authenticity, of masters of prayer who can, by their life and by their experience, really lead others into the deep awareness of God in Jesus. I learned to meditate with a man who was not a Christian but he certainly believed in God – *knew* God – and, as I read to you from the Upanishads the other evening, he had a deeply vital sense of God dwelling within him. Now it may be significant that it was not until 15 years after I learned to meditate with him that I began dimly to understand what my master had taught me and to understand the incredible richness of its full exposition in the Christian vision. This was when I studied the doctrine of the indwelling of the Holy Spirit with Dom Cyprian Vagaggini in Rome.

Not having a master or teacher can, in many cases I think, hold you up on your pilgrimage or cause you to stay longer on side-roads or dead-ends than seems necessary. And there is a very great advantage for anyone starting to meditate to do so with a master who by his own complete commitment, creates an atmosphere of seriousness and communicates a spirit of perseverance: both of which are of great importance to anyone setting out on this path.

Question: Is there a posture that is a good one for meditating?

Dom John: I think, if you can manage it, that the best way to meditate is to meditate with the spine upright. This recommendation seems to be the universal factor in all traditions. And whether you do that by kneeling, or by sitting in a chair or on the floor, or by sitting in the perfect posture or the lotus position, is a matter of personal preference, if not to say personal possibility! In our monastery at Ealing, the young men who join us for a period of six months at a time, usually adopt either the perfect posture or the lotus position: that is, they sit in a cross-legged way on the floor. I'm afraid

I'm not able to emulate them myself and I sit in a chair. But sit upright.

The importance of a posture, I think, is this: that this form of meditation is one that leads you to a complete relaxation and at the same time a total attention.

Walter Hilton, again, is very clear on this point. We have, he says, to bring ourselves into a complete unity in which we pass beyond the limitations of our bodiliness and discover total liberty. And St. Teresa says something similar when she advises us to choose a comfortable way of praying so that you are not distracted by your body. Now to be completely relaxed and completely aware is something that most of us in the West have very little experience of. We are either relaxed and about to go to sleep or watching a ballgame, chewing gum or something like that; *or* we are completely aware with all our adrenalin pumping around the system. And what you've got to learn to do is to combine these two states of consciousness. You therefore need a comfortable and yet alert position.

Question: Could you say something more about our attitude to the "word" or its function or how we could think about it?.

Dom John: The art of meditation consists in saying the mantra. It is simple but demanding. The truly simple is rarely *easy*.

When we were starting in London I went to see a friend of mine who is a Ramakrishna monk. He said, "Well, I'm very interested to see that you Catholics are now going to teach people to meditate. Now tell me exactly what you're going to tell them." And so I told him roughly what I've told you: Sit down, sit erect, say the mantra and that's it. And he said to me: "Father John that is exactly our tradition of meditating that we have from Ramakrishna himself through Swami Vivekananda. But if you tell that to a group of Westerners they just won't believe you because it will seem too simple. Now what I advise you to do is to complicate the thing a bit. So when the people come out tell them that you have some esoteric knowledge that has been handed on through the monastic order, through John Cassian, say, that's a nice-sounding name and people will be interested. But this knowledge is of such importance, you must tell them that you can't give it to them until they've been coming to your meditation centre for at least 10 weeks or something of this kind. And then, finally, you can initiate them into the thing." And indeed the Trancendental Meditation people do something rather like this.

My friend had certainly seen the major problem most Westerners face in meditation: just believing in its essential simplicity. Now saying the mantra is simplicity itself and there is nothing at all complex about the technique. But just to describe the course it takes for most people I can tell you this: Most of us start saying the mantra in the head. And we say: Ma-ra-na-tha. In my experience of teaching people over the years I find that most people have to say the mantra like that for some considerable time. But then, following Cassian's injunction to keep the mantra always before you – as you go to bed at night, as you wake in the morning, as you go down to your prayer, always preparing for your meditation – the mantra begins to take root. Then it begins, as it were, to *sound* in the heart and so you begin then almost to *feel* the mantra at a much more central level of your being. You could say that at this stage, the second you might call it, you *hear* the mantra. The third stage is when you begin to *listen* to the mantra and it's only then that your meditation is really beginning; when you are beginning to listen. My teacher used to say this to me: "When you get to this listening stage it's as though you are toiling up a mountainside and the mantra is sounding in the valley down below you. The higher you mount, the fainter becomes the sound of the mantra. And then there comes the day when the mantra is out of earshot altogether."

Now I tell you that for your encouragement. Because although it has been such a pleasure for me to be with you I have unfortunately to move on tomorrow. But I must warn you that you must approach meditation with utter simplicity. You can't be reflecting: "What stage am I at now? Am I saying the mantra? Am I sounding the mantra? Am I listening to the mantra? Or how far up the Mountainside have I got? Will it stop this day in two weeks?"

All you have to do is to just say the mantra in utter simplicity and with utter faithfulness. Without expectation "For hope would be hope for the wrong thing" as Eliot put it. Our justification for so doing will be found in remembering the words of St. Paul: "The Spirit of him who raised Jesus from the dead dwells within you and will give new life to your mortal body".

Question: What do you advise people in the way of preparing for their meditation?

Dom John: The condition of the people who come to us is, of course, very varied. Some, for example, live alone, some are fathers and mothers of large families, and so forth. But what I urge them all to do if they possibly can is to meditate first thing in the morning, that is, before the distractions of the day have overtaken them. For the majority of the people who come to meditate with us this means that they get up half an hour or so before the rest of the family and meditate at that time of greatest silence in their environment. As regards the second meditation most really have to do the best they can. What I do urge all of them and what I think the process of meditation shows them anyway (I think this is the universal testimony of our prayer groups) is that when they have been meditating for a period of six months or so they begin to look at their lives by a different set of values.

They all say that they find the quality of their life is itself beginning to change. Whereas before they would be prepared to spend a large segment of time idly watching television they now begin to think that time is a much more precious thing. And instead they might read the New Testament, some book I have recommended to their group – in any event something more serious.

I would say that generally the best immediate preparation for a meditation session is a period of silence or perhaps of listening to music. Cassian put it succinctly in the first of Abbot Isaac's Conferences: "What we want to find ourselves like while we are praying, that we ought to prepare ourselves to be before the time of prayer".

Question: How does meditation fit in with the monastic ascesis?

Dom John: The common factor is poverty. The answer to the question is, as I was suggesting to you last night, that all the external observances of the monastic life, all the discipline St. Benedict enjoins, is simply to head us in this direction, simply to prepare us for this central ascesis right at the core of our being. In many ways it's easy enough to practice community poverty, it's easy enough to practice obedience, it's easy enough to practice chastity. All these things call for a great deal but they are, from one point of view, in the external realm. And it's only when we interiorise the whole of our ascesis that our life is really beginning to take on meaning. And if you can learn to practice poverty, to practice obedience and to practice chastity right at the core of your being, in your own heart, then I believe that you are at the very heart of the monastic ascesis in this fidelity to the radical simplicity of the mantra.

And so I think it is a form of prayer that is peculiarly suitable for monks because there is both essential poverty and essential simplicity: the poverty and simplicity of one word. There is the essential chastity: the whole of your being devoted to the Lord. There is the essential obedience: *obaudire,* listening for the Master to speak. And, again, I think it is only if you can practice that total renunciation, what John of the Cross calls the total "annihilation", it is only then that your full identity, your full reality comes forward. And that full reality is that you are created by God, redeemed by Jesus and are a temple of the Holy Spirit.

Question: Do you have anything to say about handling distractions in this type of prayers

Dom John: It is the way *par excellence* to handle distractions because the purpose of the one word is simply to bring your mind to peace, silence and concentration. Not to bring it to rest with holy thoughts alone but to transcend what we know as thought altogether. And the mantra, serving this end, is like a plough that goes through your mind pushing everything else aside – "making the rough places plain". You remember what Cassian said of its "casting off and rejecting the rich and ample matter of all manner of thoughts". It is because the mind is "light and wandering", as susceptible to thoughts and images as a feather to the slightest breeze, that Cassian enjoins the mantra as the way to transcend distraction and attain stability.

The essence, the art of saying the mantra is: to say it, to sound it, to listen to it and just to ignore the distractions. Give primacy to the mantra above all else. Gradually, as you persevere in saying the mantra, the distractions do become less and less of a reality. My teacher used to say that the first three aims that you have when you begin to meditate are these: first of all, just to say the mantra for the full period of your meditation. That's your first goal and that might take a year, it might take 10 years. The second goal is to say your mantra and be perfectly calm in the face of all distractions that come. And the third preliminary aim is to say the mantra for the full time of your meditation with no distractions.

Question: What about prayer of petition and prayer of intercession? How do they fit in with this sort of prayer?

Dom John: Yes, that is a very topical question and an important one. I think that a lot of people see meditation as a kind of stoic exercise in which you are concerned with your own growth in holiness or in wisdom to the exclusion of all other relationships and concerns. It is necessary to understand clearly that meditative prayer is not the only form of prayer there is. As I have said, vocal and liturgical prayer forms both have their proper place.

But when we come to meditate we open ourselves *fully* to God's abiding presence within us, in the simple faith that that presence is the All-in-all. Our hearts are fully open to this love. And our hearts are, of course, fully open also to his scrutiny. He knows exactly all our concerns, all our loves, all our fears before we articulate them. And in this well-called "prayer of faith" we do not articulate them but offer them to him in faithful silence. A person who meditates, then, is not some heartless pursuer of wisdom but a follower of Christ who comes to him who is the fount and source of all love, who comes to be filled with that love and thereby to mediate it. We do, truly, mediate the fruit of our meditation.

Question: How should we say the mantra – what sort of speed and frequency?

Dom John: Meditation is above all the prayer of simplicity. We must therefore, each one of us, learn to be natural and to allow natural processes to unfold themselves in their own time. So, we each find our own speed for saying the mantra. Most people say it in rhythm with their breathing. The important thing is to articulate it clearly in the silence of your mind, a silence that is itself deepening and spreading all the time, and to concentrate on it to the exclusion of all other thoughts. Remember: you begin saying it, you then sound it in your heart and finally you come to listen to it with total attention.

As to frequency you must say the mantra for the entire time of your meditation to the rhythm you find for yourself. You will be tempted to rest on your oars, to float in some anaesthetised netherworld of your own. The way to transcend the temptation is absolute fidelity to the mantra. This is the condition of rooting it in your heart.

My dear brothers, I have loved being with you. Thank you very much for your kindness and wonderful hospitality. I shall always remember with great affection these days among you.

DOM JOHN MAIN (1926-1982)

John Main was born in London to Irish parents January 21st, 1926. He was educated by the Jesuits and at Westminster Choir School. He served in the army in the closing days of the war and then entered a religious order and studied in Rome. He left this order and returned to Ireland where he studied law at Trinity College Dublin and then joined the British Colonial Service. While working as a Chinese translator in Malaya he met the Indian monk who first introduced him to meditation. Returning to Europe he became a professor of Law in Dublin until he became a Benedictine monk in 1957 at Ealing Abbey in London. He studied theology in Rome, and then taught at Benedictine schools in England and the United States until his rediscovery of the Christian teaching on meditation in the works of John Cassian. In 1975 he opened the first Christian Meditation Centre and soon after accepted the invitation from the Archbishop of Montreal to found a Benedictine community there dedicated to the teaching and practice of meditation. He died there December 30th, 1982.

THE WORLD COMMUNITY FOR CHRISTIAN MEDITATION

After John Main's death the seeds of community in the practice of meditation among growing numbers of people around the world began to germinate. There are now meditation groups meeting weekly in more than sixty countries. A quarterly newsletter unites meditators in more than a hundred countries. There are twenty-five Christian Meditation Centres, some with small residential communities. The Community is served by a Guiding Board and an International Centre in London. The annual John Main Seminar and retreats worldwide deepen the journey of meditation for many. A School for Teachers helps people to share the teaching simply and effectively with others. The Community's publishing company, Medio Media, specialises in the field of the contemplative traditions. For further information please write to the International Centre or visit the Community web page at *www.wccm.org*.

THE WORLD COMMUNITY FOR CHRISTIAN MEDITATION

The World Community for Christian Meditation
International Centre
23 Kensington Square
London, W8 5HN
United Kingdom
Tele: 44 171 937 4679   Fax: 44 171 937 6790
E-mail: *wccm@compuserve.com*

In the United States
World Community
193 Wilton Road West
Ridgefield, CT 06877
203 438 2440
e-mail: pgulick@cwix.com

Visit The World Community for Christian Meditation Web site for information, weekly meditation group readings and discussion at: *www.wccm.org*

Medio Media

Medio Media is the publishing arm of the World Community for Christian Meditation. It is committed to the dissemination of the teaching of meditation in the Christian tradition and, in particular, to the work of John Main. It is further committed to the growing dialogue among meditators and seekers of all traditions based on the experience of silence common to all religions.

To obtain a copy of the complete catalog of all Medio Media Christian Meditation resource material: call 1-800-324-8305 or to order and view complete catalog visit our web site at *www.mediomedia.com* or to contact Medio Media by email: *meditation@mediomedia.com*

Medio Media Distribution Centres

Medio Media
15930 N. Oracle Road
Suite 196
Tucson, AZ 85739
1 520 825 4560

Christian Meditation Community
1283 Moffat Ave.
Verdun Quebec H4H1Z1
Canada
1 514 766 0475

Monastery of Christ The King
29 Bramley Road, London N14 4He
United Kingdom
+181 440 7769

Christian Meditation Centre
58 Meadow Grove
Blackrock Cork
Ireland
+353 21 357249

Medio Media Distribution Centres *(cont'd)*

Centro Di Meditazione Cristiana
Abbazia Di San Miniato
Via Delle Porte Sante 34
50125 Firenze
Italy
+390 41 21 824 1149

Christeluk Meditatie Centrum
Beiaardlaam1
Grimbergen 1850
Belgium
+32 2 2695071

Christian Meditation Groups
51/1 Sedsiri Road
Bangkok 10400
Thailand
+66 2 271 3295

Christian Meditation Centre
9 Mayfield Avenue
Singapore 438023
Singapore
+65 348 6790

Christian Meditation Network (WA)
P.O. Box 323
Tuart Hill W.A. 6060
Australia
+61 8 444 5810

Christian Meditation Group
31 North Terrace
Kelburn,
Wellington 6005N2
New Zealand
+64 4 475-7847

Christian Meditation Centres

International Centre: 23 Kensington Square / London W8 5HN / United Kingdom.
Tel: +44 171 937 4679 Fax: +44 171 937 6790
E-mail: wccm@compuserve.com

Australia: Australian Christian Meditation Community / PO Box 66390 / St. Kilda Rd. Central / Victoria 3004.
Tel/Fax: +61 7 3300 3873 or +61 3 9435 8943
E-mail: acmchall@Bigpond.com

Belgium: Christelijk Meditatie Centrum / Beiaardlaan 1 / 1850 Grimbergen.
Tel/Fax: +32 2 269 5071

Brazil: Crista Meditacao Communidade / C.P. 33266 / CEP 22442-970 / Rio de Janeiro / RJ.
Tel: +55 21 512 3806 Fax: +55 21 294 7995
E-mail: smorais@ibm.net

Canada: Christian Meditation Community / PO Box 552 / Station NDG / Montreal / Quebec H4A 3P9.
Tel: +1 514 766 0475 Fax: +1 514 937 8178
E-mail: mark.schofield@sympatico.ca

Centre de Méditation Chrétienne / Cap Vie / 367 boul. Ste Rose / Laval / QC H71 1N3.
Tel/Fax: +1 514 625 0133

Germany: Zentrum für Christliche Meditation / c/o Gunter Meng / Postfach 122045 / 68071 Mannheim.
Tel: +49 171 268 6245 Fax: +49 40 3603 095 720
E-mail: GueMeng@aol.com

India: Christian Meditation Centre / 1/1429 Bilathikulam Road / Calicut / 673006 Kerala.
Tel: +91 33 495 50395

Ireland: Christian Meditation Centre / 4 Eblana Ave. / Dun Laoghaire / Co. Dublin.
Tel: +353 1 280 1505 Fax: +353 1 280 8720

Italy: Centro di Meditazione Christiana / Abbazia di San Miniato al Monte / Via Delle Porte Sante 34 / 50125 Firenze.
Tel/Fax: +39 55 247 6302

Malaysia: Christian Meditation Centre / 7 Jalan Pekaka Dua / SG. Dua / Gelogar / Pulau Pinang 11700 / Malaysia.
Tel: +60 4 657 7414   E-mail: saymooi@tm.net.my

New Zealand: Christian Meditation Centre / 31 North Terrace / Wellington 6005N2

Philippines: Christian Meditation Centre / 11 Osmeña St. / South Admiral Village / Bgy Merville / Pque. / MM 1760.
Tel: +63 2 824 9595   Fax: +63 2 823 3742

Singapore: Christian Meditation Centre / 9 Mayfield Avenue / Singapore 438 023.
Tel: +65 348 6790   Fax: +65 348 7302

Thailand: Christian Meditation Centre / 51/1 Sedsiri Road / Bangkok 10400.
Tel. +66 2 271 3295   Fax: +66 2 271 2632
E-mail: sketudat@mozart.inet.co.th

United Kingdom: Christian Meditation Centre / The Hermitage / Monastery of Christ the King / 29 Bramley Road / Cockfosters / London N14 4HE.
Tel./Fax: +44 181 441 0680
E-mail: cmcuk@compuserve.com.

United States: Christian Meditation Centre / 1080 West Irving Park Rd. / Roselle IL 60172.
Tel./Fax: +1 630 351 2613

John Main Institute / 7315 Brookville Rd. / Chevy Chase / MD 20815.
Tel: +1 301 652 8635
E-mail: wmcoerp@erols.com

Christian Meditation Centre / 1619 Wight St. / Wall / NJ 07719.
Tel: +1 732 681 6238   Fax: +1 732 280 5999
Web page editor: Greg Ryan
E-mail: gjryan@aol.com

The Cornerstone Centre / 1215 East Missouri Ave. / Suite A 100 / Phoenix AZ 85014-2914.
Tel: +1 602 279 3454   Fax: +1 602 957 3467
E-mail: ccrmjr@worldnet.att.net